A is for Amy

A is for Amy

A NOVELLA

by

Steven Crandell

2026 · Quinn, Rose, Elliot & Ellery · Duvall, Washington

Printed in the United States of America

ISBN 978-0-9789358-3-2 hardcover
ISBN 978-0-9789358-4-9 e-book

No AI was used in the creation of this book.

Published by Quinn, Rose, Elliot & Ellery
Duvall, Washington

Book design and production by Studio E Books, Santa Barbara
Cover design by Andrew Antone, AAexpressive

For Marcella Therese Novak Crandell, my mother.

Thank you for loving literature so passionately

that I could not help but love it myself.

I am only a writer today because

your life inspired me to imagine it was possible.

2005

A

ADONIS was a strange name for a milkman.

An e-milkman.

That's how he described himself. She just had to order the dairy products she wanted on the Internet, and he would be at her door within the hour, bearing all the milk, butter and fresh cream she desired.

He was at her front door right now, having knocked politely three times—not-too-loud, not-too-soft. He offered her a brochure. And while she opened it to read, he slid a business card into the big sloppy pocket of her cardigan. Her fingers instinctively followed his into the dark woolen hollow. To get the card, she thought. But she found something else.

Out of sight, their hands met. Skin touched skin. A synaptic frenzy spread up her forearm, spiking tiny fair hairs to attention. She hadn't had sex since the last time she became pregnant, hadn't kissed a male over the age of three in 15 months. Just the prospect of flirting was so unaccustomed it felt like a sky-dive.

Adonis eased his hand up and out of the pocket. She wondered if he noticed, but he betrayed nothing. He was calm—standing with excellent posture, looking in her eyes, waiting with uncommon patience. She looked down at her tiger-striped house slippers. She composed herself. Their hands had been in the well of her sweater pocket far too long, but at the same time, she admitted, not nearly long enough. However.

Amy often used that negative conjunction to end things that really weren't ended. She would think or say "however" and then drift into silence.

Amy knew life was about negative conjunctions. She was 26. But she felt 46. Over-tired, under-fulfilled. Somewhat isolated. Too isolated. Looking for something she didn't have. To be truthful, and she liked to be truthful, she showed symptoms of what could easily develop into a case of premature mid-life crisis.

She had a degree in public relations and had worked several jobs as a PR consultant. She knew how to look for the positive in any person, in any organization, in any situation. But that was public relations. Private relations had taught her the opposite lesson—that only the shadow of a negative outcome was required to contradict any plan, any hope. She knew life carried the potential for failure in its very conception.

Conception was another area in which she had some expertise. Three kids under five. She loved them dearly. And she made a point of introducing herself as an "independent mother," rather than a single mom, which invited judgement and gave a connotation of deprivation. Her kids were not deprived. But the truth was she was parenting alone.

She noticed Adonis wore a white milkman's uniform—buttoned to the neck, but made of stretchy, clingy material, a Lycra blend. His pectorals swelled to the punctuation of his nipples. He followed her eyes and immediately rubbed his chest.

"Cold for April," he said. "Should have worn my jacket."

B

Amy's husband Bart resided in a small wooden box on the mantelpiece above the fireplace. Right beside him sat a photo of Amy and the two older kids in their funeral finery. Bart's photographer brother Zachary had taken the portrait for free—as a kind of going-away present. Zachary had been moving to Philadelphia. Bart, on the other hand, had been moving to the crematorium and then to the box on the mantelpiece.

Dust to dusty. Amy hadn't cleaned there in months.

Bart died while Amy was 6 months pregnant with their third child. It was tragic timing, but there were some pluses. Death had cured his chronic snoring. The grocery bill was way down. And there were fewer interruptions when Amy spoke.

Before his demise, he wouldn't let her finish a sentence. A real estate salesman. A talker. He used to say that in his game, you had to establish yourself with image and words. You had to give your customers a handle to grab.

So it made sense that Bart was attracted to pretty much anyone who would grab his handle. There were motel rooms rented by the hour. There were certain stupid females. And males.

Anyone willing to get within a quarter-mile of Bart's pecker was stupid. Like Amy, for example. However.

To be fair, Bart did have his attractive side. She appreciated it most when he had his back turned. He claimed he could balance a flute glass of champagne on the nearly horizontal shelf of his upper derriere. She doubted this, but she had witnessed a marshmallow poised on top of either cheek.

Bart had abandoned his life and his family in a public way. He caught a taxi on a business trip to LA and asked the driver to stop on a bridge over Interstate 5. Then he took a leap into the freeway traffic. Whether or not he intended it, he landed in the car-pool lane—thus not compounding suicide with unnecessary mutilation. It was rush-hour. The other four lanes were grid-locked.

A Ford Explorer, with four people inside, slammed on its brakes. The Explorer missed running him over by two SUV lengths. Meanwhile, the cabbie scrambled down the embankment and rushed onto the freeway to pull Bart to the shoulder. People thought the cabbie was a hero, but Bart was already dead. The cabbie went through Bart's pockets looking for the fare. He found a toothbrush, two condoms, a wallet filled with business cards and loose change. No photos of his family. No suicide note. And no folding money.

Bart's child was born three months later. Amy named her Bartlette. People always asked. Amy always told them. Nothing to do with the pear.

For her, it was just a way of saying goodbye to Bart and forgiving him all at once. He was a shit. That was a fact. But his third baby was cute as a button, and Amy liked the idea that a corrupt man might have his name redeemed by an innocent child. However.

A few weeks ago, on the first anniversary of Bart's death, Amy's friend Eustazia sent her a book. *Passionate Marriage*, by Dr. David Schnarch. Amy called her straight back and told her it was a nasty, mean joke. Eustazia, "U" to her friends, took offense. The book wasn't mean, nasty or a joke. After all, Amy might meet somebody. This book would leave her prepared.

"There's always hope," U said.

"There's always suicide," said Amy.

She waited a few seconds before she laughed.

Baby Bartlette just smiled and smiled. She was a happy baby.

C

Adonis wasn't his real name. Duh. That was the downside. The upside was, she liked his real name better: Charlie.

Charlie, the e-milkman, had brought her some cream cheese. He had brought it by as a free trial. She explained that she didn't even have an Internet connection. He maintained that a butter knife would work fine.

When she smiled, he said she could use the telephone to order anything if she wanted.

All this at the door to her home. Him, looking like his pseudonym. Her, feeling delightfully tingly and thoroughly ill at ease.

"It's a free promotion," he said. He offered the cream cheese to her again. It came in a thick foil bag with a scarlet "e" on the front. She took it, and then, in a fit of inspired composure, she asked him if he was thirsty. She had not blushed. And he may not have noticed her eyelids fluttering from nervousness like butterfly wings.

It was his time to waver. He looked at his watch, which was enormous—with enough dials and numbers to be NASA standard equipment. He looked at the clipboard he carried in his other hand.

Clearly, he had a schedule to keep.

"It's a free invitation," she said.

He smiled and said he would love a quick coffee.

Of course, it was strange to invite a strange man in for coffee, particularly when the kids were home. But then, they were always home.

And Charlie didn't seem strange: more comfortable than anything else; straight; honest; open. Hell, Bart spent time with the kids and he was none of those things.

So she introduced him to her children and sat him down in the living room. Then, picking up baby Bartlette, she retreated gracefully to the kitchen, leaving the door open to watch how things developed in the living room.

Charlie kneeled down to the kids' blocks and immediately started asking them about what they were building. Mmmm, impressive. In reality, most men were children, but not so many would get down on the floor to play when they themselves were in a hurry. Charlie seemed to have some other orientation—an inner dimension to go with his outer ones.

She spread the cream cheese on a toasted bagel and then held the knife out and stared at it. It seemed a waste to leave the cream cheese there. So she imagined licking it off his shoulder, right where all the smooth bands of muscle joined together like tracks running into a central train station. Shifting baby Bartlette to her high chair, she opened the fridge to put away the cream cheese. Then, using the fridge door as a screen to the living room, she put her tongue to the spreading knife and slowly ran it from shank to point. With her eyes shut. The cream cheese was rich and tangy.

"Bad manners, Mommy," Carmen said. "No licking the knife." Her four-and-a-half-year-old, Carmen, had slipped away from the blocks, sneaking up under the fridge door to observe.

Amy swallowed the cream cheese and put down the knife. She crouched down to reassure her eldest daughter. Mommy had forgotten. Mommy would not lick a sharp thing like that again. It was dangerous.

When she emerged with her bagels, a plunger of coffee and a pitcher of fresh cream, she hit her first obstacle. Charlie refused to eat the cream cheese. He scraped it off. He was on a diet, he said. And this milkman took his coffee black.

She watched his stomach muscles ridge and disappear through the figure-hugging Lycra of his shirt as he sat up to take the steaming cup.

Amy thanked God she wasn't wearing Lycra. She felt her extra pounds bulge at her side—like stuffing escaping from a worn-out sofa. The breast-feeding hadn't slimmed her down like after the other two pregnancies.

Amy tried to sit straight and sylph-like. Posture mattered. The outer semblance of the inner self.

Alas, she looked down and caught a glimpse of her thick ankles which led to her sturdy (big) legs and her sturdier (bigger) hips. Hippo, she thought. From the waist down—I'm a hippo.

She was exaggerating. Accentuating the negative.

She wasn't anything like a hippo. However.

She lowered her bagel. The poisoned chalice. Suddenly, she didn't feel hungry.

Charlie sensed her hesitance. He smiled like sunshine. "Eat up," he said.

In the years BC (Before Children), her figure had been something she enjoyed.

That was when she was Amy Dellaconta, not Amy Franklin. Then, she made an appealing female landscape—valleys to go with her hills. Then, she had a waist.

At age 20, even on a bad day, she looked Rubensesque. On a good day, with the right light, she could rise up out of a seashell right alongside the Venus de Milo.

Her number one physical attribute, though, was her hair. Thick, with lazy curls. The color of maple syrup. Flowing down, down to the middle of her back. Bart said he used to get hard just running his hands though her hair. But now she was going gray. She plucked out five offending hairs yesterday.

"You're healthy and you've certainly got a glossy coat," said Charlie, reading her mind and easing it all at once. "But you still need your calcium. Cream cheese is a good source."

The kids edged higher on her like an incoming tide. Bartlette whimpered and reached for her breast. Amy knew she didn't look great, but at that moment it ceased to matter so much. Charlie had noticed her hair. A small thing. Insignificant to the point of being unrecognizably trivial to someone else. After all, she was under no illusions here. As usual, ultimate defeat was expected. However.

She took a bite of the cream cheese.

Charlie nodded to Bartlette and winked at Amy. "Go ahead. I don't mind."

She hesitated. She explained she normally waited till Carmen and Ferguson were down for their naps. Otherwise, it was too hard, too many distractions.

He told her to go for it. He said he would take care of the kids. He said he had a lullaby.

He pulled a CD from his delivery bag, walked into the living room, and stuck it in the stereo. Hot, fast salsa music. Some lullaby. But he winked at Amy and turned down the volume in deference to her imminent breast-feeding.

"Do you mind if I take off my shirt?"

Her eyebrows went to the penthouse. "Interesting question," she said.

He sighed and smiled at the same time. It was a disarming smile. He paused the music and walked back to her. Then he explained that being an e-milkman was just a day job. He was in career transition. He used to be an x-ray technician. Good money, bad vibes, he said. He shrugged. His real dream was to become a dancer-choreographer. An exotic dancer-choreographer. He blushed a little. He waited for her to laugh or to ask if he was serious. She did neither. Instead, she shrugged. "Sure," she said. "Take it off."

He burst out laughing, then whipped off the shirt in one movement. He stood before her, waiting quietly.

His six-pack had the hills and valleys of a human relief map.

She tried to remain the picture of calm, but her face probably told another story.

He noticed but said nothing. Their eyes connected. There was a moment. Was it that she didn't pigeon-hole him? Was it that he was sincere about his "exotic" ambitions? Or was it something else? Amy wasn't sure.

"What's *your* dream?" he said.

She was stunned. It was a logical thing to ask, of course. It was just…well, she couldn't remember if anyone had ever asked her that question. Certainly no one since Carmen was born.

"Besides being a mom, I mean." He smiled that smile again. Charming. Real. Distabilizingly genuine.

She flushed bright red. She felt seen. In a positive way, of course, but still…she mumbled something, stumbling for words. She knew the answer to his question. She'd known for a long time. But she'd kept it to herself. Like a dangerous, potentially embarrassing secret.

"I…I want to be a teacher… a teacher who makes students laugh." She looked down and found a little composure. "You've heard of English Lit? I'm going to teach English Laughter."

"Ni-i-i-ce," he said. He stood straight as a ballerino and elegantly ran his arms through the first 3 *port de bra* positions, ending with a deep bow. Then he straightened. "I'd take your class, Prof. *You* have a good sense of humor."

He deftly pivoted back to the stereo and pushed play.

Slowly, his ballet formality dissolved, and he began to gyrate and undulate his abdomen to the music. He began to parry and thrust. The kids, including Bartlette, were fascinated. Charlie's abs could do the wave in sequence just like the fans at Dodger Stadium.

After a few moments, though, Bartlette's hunger took control. She tugged at her mother's shirt. Amy shot a glance at Charlie as she positioned Bartlette on her breast, to see if he had caught a glimpse of her own milk delivery system. But he was dancing. So Bartlette clamped on, and the rest of the family watched the Charlie show.

Ferguson was especially taken with Charlie. Of course, Amy was aware that the three-year-old was sorely lacking in male role models. She watched her little boy. She watched him stand up and try to move his hips in the same outlandish orbit that Charlie's circumscribed. She wondered if promiscuity was genetic or learned.

D

Three reasons why Amy was a fool:

1. She'd just ordered ice cream from Charlie—at three times the price she'd normally pay in the supermarket.
2. She was mildly allergic to most dairy food. Anything made with cow's milk could trigger her asthma and sometimes give her a rash.
3. Charlie couldn't make the delivery. He said his friend would bring it over.

Now Danielle stood in her doorway. Flat stomach, thin smile. Tanned and punctured in all the fashionable spots. Something resembling a silver railroad spike had been driven through her navel. She wore hip-hugging workout shorts and a purple acid-wash jog bra. Her hair was acid-wash, too.

She unzipped an insulated backpack, pulling out approximately 3,200 calories worth of frozen dessert. "Wow," she said. "Binge night, huh?"

Amy was stunned by the rudeness, but she recovered quickly. "I'm having a birthday party for one of my children." It was a lie. But Danielle swallowed it. She handed over the ice cream and crouched down to talk to Ferguson.

"Your birthday, big guy?"

Ferguson ran away. Danielle shrugged, "Not a ladies man, huh?"

Amy gave her the money. "He's just disappointed he didn't get to see Charlie," said Amy. "He thought he might get to dance."

"Yeah," said Danielle. "His glutes rock." Danielle was chewing gum at a rapid pace, pausing between chews to let her words escape.

Ferguson returned carrying a used diaper. He stood for a moment and then dropped it on Danielle's running shoes. Danielle jumped back like the diaper carried the plague. The diaper jumped with her. Panicked, she kicked her foot wildly. The diaper landed in the driveway—five yards away.

In that moment, Amy realized she not only deeply loved, but also deeply admired her son.

"Sorry," Amy said, picking up the diaper with her bare hand. "But at least it wasn't one of the poopy ones."

Danielle left in a hurry.

THAT night, Carmen asked Amy about dandelions. Which was the real dandelion? She wanted to know. The plant with the long green leaves? The yellow flower? Or the round thing with helicopter seeds that you blew into the sky?

Amy explained. Dandelions were like people. They changed while they grew. So the leaves, the flower and the seeds were all dandelions. Just different stages.

Amy told Carmen she was the long green leaves before the flower came. Carmen got angry. She said she wanted to be the flower, too. Amy smiled and reassured her daughter that she was the flower, and the seeds, as well. Amy said the flower and the seeds were inside the leaves, nature's magic just hadn't brought them out yet. Wait, she said, and you'll see, Carmen. You'll be a flower one day. When the time's right.

Carmen thought about this for a while and then asked if she were the dandelion's leaves, what was Amy?

Amy looked down and pictured the bald head of a dandelion denuded of seeds.

I'm not sure, sweetheart, she said.

When she looked up. Carmen had already left to play.

E

Ed Ramses telephoned from Bart's old real estate office. "You can call me Ed," he said. He wanted Amy's e-mail address. He said he was cleaning out Bart's old computer files to make some room on the hard disc, and he had come across "this e-mail" which she might want to see. Ed hadn't read it, of course. Private correspondence. Well, at least he hadn't read all of it. You know how you have to read a little bit of things to know whether they're worth saving? Anyway, knowing how Bart was deceased and everything, Ed thought Amy might want to see this, this e-mail. It was an eye-opener. Ed had to admit that much. He didn't have a clue that Bart was unfaithful. With men as well as women. "Wow," said Ed. "Kept that completely hidden."

The silence on the phone line grew to the size of a football field or the Grand Canyon or the Pacific Frigging Ocean.

Amy said she didn't have an e-mail address. Or the Internet. Or a god-damn computer for that matter.

Ed wondered about a fax.

Amy said she had a mailbox.

Ed said the e-mail was short, and he would be glad to read it over the phone. If she liked.

Amy told him to do her a favor. First, print out the e-mail. Then, roll it into a tube. And finally, use it to perform a colonic irrigation on himself.

She hung up in anger.

The phone rang seconds later. It was Ed. He said he was sorry. Really sorry, in fact. But it was a practical thing, and he had to ask: Had she thought about putting her house on the market and moving to a condo? She probably didn't need so much room, and the mortgage payments had to be tough without Bart's salary, and there were a lot of sharks out there.

She screamed as loud as she could into the receiver. Then she hung up again.

She was pissed. Really pissed, in fact.

So, she sat down and took five slow in-breaths, breathing out even more slowly. Just like yoga.

Unfortunately, Ed did have a point.

She went to her desk drawer to pull out the latest statement from the bank. Just to reassure herself. In her "emergency" account, the one she had built up before she met Bart, there was enough to cover mortgage and expenses. Except paid child care, of course. Enough for 13 months. Pretty good, she thought. Lots of time to figure out next steps while I care for my kids. Right?

Yes.

Kind of.

However.

Back at the office, Ed shook his head in bewilderment. Then he remembered to write down her name a week ahead in his daily planner. For a follow-up call. Ed knew she might change her mind about selling.

Two days later, Bart's suicide note arrived in the mail. Ed had added his business card in the mailing, not to mention a fridge magnet decorated with his three phone numbers, his e-mail address and his photo.

F

Bart was a dick. However.

Amy sat down with his last e-mail in the privacy of her bedroom. She had bribed Ferguson and Carmen not to bother her. A box of chocolate chip fudge cookies did the trick. Baby Bartlette was sleeping. Amy left the door ajar to hear any child emergency-distress calls she might have to respond to. Then she settled in for a good, solid half-hour of loathing.

No one is so deserving of hate as someone who you once loved.

The e-mail said this:

> Babe,
>
> You may never get this.
>
> Which is okay.
>
> I wanted to clear my conscience before I died. And I didn't want to take the risk that you might not forgive me.
>
> So, for the hell of it, here are my top six regrets.

1. You know that life insurance policy I kept talking about getting? I didn't. (My bad.)
2. You used to look hot in a bikini. You don't anymore. (Your bad.)
3. I visited hookers while on road trips. (I think you knew about this.)
4. Not all the hookers were female.
5. I won't be around for the kids. (Tell them I love them anyway.)
6. My horses kept losing. (Their bad.)

That's about it, Babe.

Oh, and don't freak out too much about why I did it. It's just that my life kind of went into escrow and never came out. And weighing up the pluses and the minuses, choosing the time of my death just came out a lot more attractive than having it done at someone else's convenience.

I don't know if I ever told you this but I'm majorly in debt to a couple of dudes with big forearms and small brains, who seem to suffer from some kind of aggressive–compulsive disorder.

Anyway.

Babe, I know this is going to be a shock. But don't take my suicide personally. As much as I'd like to blame it on you, it's not your fault.

Goodbye (forever),

Bart

Amy put down the e-mail. This was the man she had married. Selfish. Insensitive. Childish. A liar. A cheater. An asshole. A jerk. A coward. And most of all, a lousy husband and father. Reading the black words on the white paper now, they seemed hardly credible. But the voice in the words was his—full of himself and his games to the bitter end.

She did the books at their house and she knew how much he earned and how much he spent on the horses. As for the idea that burly loan sharks had been about to kill Bart, it was just another fanciful lie, a way for him to avoid admitting that he was giving up on himself and his family.

On the front porch of death, Bart was just the same as he was in the living room of life. Weak. Amy found this consistency both comforting and soul-destroying. It was soul-destroying because Bart was proof of her spectacularly poor taste in choosing a mate. It was comforting because, even if she tried, it would be difficult to choose as poorly again.

Just then, she had a moment of insight. And though she normally shook her head when she thought about her life, she found herself nodding.

Bart's e-mail had done something extraordinary. She felt free. After 15 months spent squashed in the trash compactor of grief and guilt, she realized it didn't matter anymore why he did it. In fact, he didn't matter anymore. He was history. Their relationship was history.

She was the present.

It felt like bravado, like a cover for some seriously deep insecurity, but she liked the feeling anyway.

She was free. She could choose.

Amy sat up as straight as she could on the former marital, now widowed, water bed. She examined herself in the long mirror opposite. She eased her hands under her breasts, then lifted them and the old nursing bra that housed them, to a pre-motherhood altitude.

Time to get perky, she thought.

G

COSMETIC surgery was out of the question. Too expensive. For that matter, so was a new bra.

However.

If you could take out a mortgage to pay for something as mundane as shelter, you certainly could add to your Visa debt in order to turn your life around.

Or you could ask Mom.

Grace Dellaconta was a big woman with a big heart and a bigger mouth. She loved her daughter a lot. But listening was not her strong suit. Amy had learned to create situations where there were natural limits on any conversation. Otherwise, she could drown in her mother's words.

A lot was riding on this bra-buying expedition, so Amy planned well in advance. The kids were central to the strategy. First, Amy told Grace about her insight, about being able to choose her direction in life. Then she revealed her first choice—the perkification of her boobs.

Mother approved. Buying new underwear was an important developmental milestone in life. It started at puberty and continued through gaining weight, losing weight, getting pregnant, nursing children, finishing nursing, *et cetera*, *et cetera*. At each stage of womanhood, new underwear was a new foundation. So to speak.

Grace could be pretty profound when it came to lace, elastic and foam. Amy had to interrupt, though, to get to the point. It wasn't so much her need, but her neediness.

This was really a form of begging from a blood relative, but Amy preferred to think of it as a way her mother and she could feel closer without having to spend much time together.

In any case, Grace was more than happy to pay.

Then Amy asked for one more favor.

"Of course, darling," said Grace.

"Would you watch the kids while I go shopping?"

This was the trickiest bit because Grandma didn't like being Grandma while the kids were still kids. When Carmen was born, Grace promised to do lots of things with her as soon as she was a little older. How old? Amy asked. "Eighteen," said Grace. Carmen was one and a half when Amy discovered that her grandmother meant 18 years, not months.

Grace's reasoning was simple: kids were too childish. Short-attention spans. Poor listeners.

Grace had quit procreating after one kid. Not that Amy ruined her first marriage or anything. Or made it hard with husbands two and three. It was just easier now that Amy was grown up. Easier to talk.

Amy could hear the disappointment in her mother's voice as she finally agreed to look after the kids. The tone of voice was meant to engender guilt, and then that guilt was meant to produce contrition and finally inspire Amy to call her back and tell her she didn't have to watch the kids after all.

Fat chance.

Amy put down the telephone and smiled. She looked at her children. They seemed so happy. Carmen was trying to dress up Bartlette to match Space Shuttle Barbie by using aluminum foil, glitter glue and Amy's bathing cap. Meanwhile, Ferguson had taken off his shirt and was dancing to the CD of Latin music that Charlie/Adonis had left behind. Ferguson frowned with concentration while he moved his hips to the rhythm. The pre-school salsa stripper.

Amy shook her head. She loved her kids so very much. Almost as much as she loved the idea of an afternoon away from them.

You see, Amy had kept a little information from her mother.

She wasn't shopping alone.

H

"THE last man to make love to me is dead now, too," Eustazia said.

She was trying to cheer up Amy even though Amy was already feeling happy. This made no sense at all—except if you were Eustazia.

U to her friends.

You see, U had a deep desire to sympathize with people who were worse off than she was. It was a win-win. She felt better about her own life—i.e. superior—while also appearing understanding, caring and other-oriented.

Amy, of course, understood this, and knew that one of the best ways of showing she cared about U was to go along with her sympathetic thing.

"Remember Pierre?" U said.

Amy remembered, but she pretended not to hear. She had her nose in a book by the Dalai Lama (and a shrink named Howard C. Cutler) called *The Art of Happiness: A Handbook for Living.*

The two friends stood in the bookstore at the mall, having already achieved massive shopping success. U had taken Amy to the lingerie factory outlet store where she'd picked up a glam black bra that held her breasts up while pushing them together. U said Amy looked like a young Sophia Loren without a tan. That only took $20 of the hundred bucks that Grace had donated. So they went to lunch, drank too much wine and were now thinking how they could spend the last $30.

"Remember Pierre?" said U again.

Amy answered without looking up. "The guy in the wheelchair?"

"He was only paralyzed from the knees down," said U.

I believe that the very purpose of our life is to seek happiness, wrote the Dalai Lama.

"Cool," said Amy, more to the Dalai Lama than U.

U frowned and punched Amy in the arm. "No it wasn't," U said. "It was kind of disgusting. Pierre's breath tasted like roll-your-own cigarettes and fermented licorice. But he had only four weeks to live. It was mercy sex."

I believe that happiness can be achieved through training of the mind, Amy read in the book.

Amy looked up at U, straight in her eyes. "Pierre did have a sexy voice," she said.

"It wasn't like that," said U.

"What was it like?"

"Like having sex with a stranger, with someone you didn't love."

"So?" Amy went back to her book.

"So now he's dead, gone forever, and I'll never have a chance to know him better, to get close to him."

"To have sex with him again," said Amy with a smile. "Must have been good."

By bringing about a certain inner discipline, we can undergo a transformation of our attitude, our entire outlook and approach to living.

"That's not the point," said U.

Amy looked at her again. For the sympathetic one, U demanded a lot of TLC.

"Sorry, what's the point?"

"The point is, now I know how you feel. With Bart being your last sex partner and everything. It must be hard for you."

Amy looked down and read more of the Dalai Lama's book:

When we speak of this inner discipline, it can of course involve many things, many methods. But generally speaking, one begins by identifying those factors which lead to happiness and those factors which lead to suffering. Having done this, one then sets about gradually eliminating those factors which lead to suffering and cultivating those which lead to happiness. That is the way.

Amy nodded, still looking down.

U touched her shoulder. "I understand," U said.

Amy bought the Dalai Lama book and one for her mother called *How to Talk So Kids Will Listen & Listen So Kids Will Talk*. She also purchased gifts for everyone. For Bartlette, a rubber hippo for the bath that spat from the front and peed from the back. For Ferguson, a CD called *Hot Salsa Hits #4*. For Carmen, a Barbie Rescue Helicopter Emergency set. And for U, she bought a navy blue beret in honor of the dead—but not forgotten—Pierre. In honor of what might have been.

Of course, it all cost more than $30. So she mortgaged her Visa and promised herself she'd find a job soon. Or win the lottery.

I

Amy returned to bedlam. Carmen and Ferguson were engaged in hand-to-hand combat over Ibey the rubber ibex. Ferguson wanted to behead him, and Carmen wanted to save him from that fate so he could be her two-horned unicorn in a special parade of dolls. Bartlette was teething on the television remote control while poop dribbled out of her filled diaper.

Christmas wrapping paper covered the floor. (It had been the ocean.) CDs had been taken out of their cases and piled high in a tower. (It had been the lighthouse.) The kid-size plastic table had been turned upside-down in the middle of the room. (It had been the boat—with teak salad servers as paddles.) But that game had been forgotten now for the battle over Ibey.

In the kitchen, oblivious to the child chaos, sat Grace. She flicked through a magazine and talked on the telephone.

The cost of freedom, thought Amy. However.

Once order was restored and presents distributed, domestic tranquility returned. Everybody loved their gifts. Grace mistakenly thought her book was called *How to*

Make People Listen While You Talk. She thought it was the best thing ever and said she'd read it as soon as she got home.

When the taxi arrived, Amy said goodbye and closed the door on her smiling mother.

Then she picked up her Dalai Lama book and stared at the title page.

She noticed that " i " was smack dab in the middle of "happiness."

Then she sat down in the middle of the upside-down plastic table, poised a wooden salad server, outrigger-style, just above the Christmas paper ocean, and shouted in her best pirate captain's voice: "Climb aboard, me maties! There be a storm a-brewin' in that thar ocean! We'll have to paddle fast!"

Carmen and Ferguson each grabbed a wooden spoon and scrambled to find a place behind Amy on the table. Sitting nearby on the floor and witnessing a game that was a staple in their house, Bartlette burbled and slapped her hands on her chubby thighs.

J

The next morning Amy went into action.

She brushed her hair a hundred times upside-down until it shined soft and mellow and voluptuous. She put on her new bra and her silky kimono robe, did her makeup, and then arranged her décolletage in the mirror so just enough was showing.

She smiled at herself. From the breasts up, she could no longer be classed as dowdy and unattractive. In fact, she was on the verge of looking good.

The purpose of life is to seek happiness. The Dalai Lama said it. Maybe that's all you had to do, she thought. Just getting the bra and having a plan made her feel light and positive. She almost didn't know herself. Maybe it wasn't the impossible dream after all. Mental training. Inner discipline. Women, mothers, teachers. They did that stuff all the time. The key was the audacity not just to want it, but to seek it out. She felt confident for the first time in years. She strode to the telephone and dialed. She wished this feeling would last forever, or at least the rest of the morning.

Instead, it lasted about as long as it took for someone to answer a phone.

Adonis didn't work for the e-dairy company anymore, the operator voice said. They didn't have anyone named Charlie on their roster either. No, they didn't have a contact number, and if they did, they couldn't give it out anyway. Privacy issues.

Danielle? No, Danielle had left their company the same day as Adonis. Sorry. They did have a special on sour cream, though.

Amy hung up and wandered into the living room where she sat down on the couch. Charlie was just a wannabe exotic choreographer, after all. An ex-x-ray technician. No great catch. Just another man.

A man who was trying to follow his dream. Brave possibly—impractical certainly. A guy with a gorgeous body, to be sure, who was lovely with her kids and treated her with respect and kindness, but who couldn't even hold down a job as a milkman. Why should she even bother?

Of course, it wasn't really about how sexy or good or reliable Charlie was. It didn't even matter that he asked her about her dream. In a way, it wasn't about Charlie at all. Exactly. However.

Ferguson noticed her staring into space and came over to stand on her feet. He asked why she was in her fancy bathrobe. When she didn't answer, he ran to get his Jack-in-the-box and opened it right into her kneecap. Still no reply. Carmen arrived and asked why Mommy's boobies were squished together. And Bartlette, not to be left out, crawled up on her and began to grizzle for a nurse, pulling at the new black bra, puzzled that it had no milk flap.

Amy took her sexy bra off and plugged in Bartlette.

Mr. Dalai Lama said: *Eliminate factors that lead to suffering and cultivate those that lead to happiness.*

What about when you cultivate happiness, but end up suffering? What about when your best efforts to live life well leave you dejected, deflated and depressed?

It was a paradox. It was also a fact of life. Amy's life.

What did the Dalai Lama know about being an independent mother anyway? The only thing they had in common was that they each had the sex life of a monk.

K

Amy was on the desperate side of midnight. Her silky kimono robe smelled of breast milk vomit. Her hair looked like a bird's nest. She felt like screaming or doing something violent, but instead she sat up and caressed Bartlette's head as she slept. There had been enough screaming for one night.

Bartlette had a crib, of course. She had been fed, of course. And burped. None of that mattered.

Wave after wave of her daughter's crying had battered Amy into capitulation. Bartlette now shared Amy's bed. It was Amy's weak spot. A child's discontent took her heart hostage. And even if she held out a long time, in the end, she gave in and paid the ransom. Stop crying. Please. Just...stop...crying. However.

Amy wobbled as she sat on the king-size water bed that Bart had insisted on getting soon after they were married. He liked the idea that they could have sex at sea, as he called it. It turned him on. "Undulate me, baby," he would say in a whisper worthy of Barry White.

However.

Basically, in spite of an excellent body, he was cringe-material as a lover. Yet right now she missed him. Once upon a time, he chose her. He loved her. It was nice to be wanted. Even more, to be cherished. If she were completely honest, she longed to be loved again. Loved with intensity. But also with mutuality.

The cycle of giving and receiving love is the key to any romantic relationship. She knew this in her bones. Love is generous. Love returns love. Multiplies love. False love is selfish and stingy and duplicitous. Ask anyone who's been cheated on.

She didn't hate Bart, though. It was just that he had the attention span of a fruit fly. Which scientists have determined to be about 4 seconds. And, as Amy discovered after her wedding, fruit flies are naturally promiscuous.

As she reflected on it now, her missing him was not about the quality of his love or companionship.

It was, instead, an indication of her current level of emotional deprivation.

Right now, water or not, the bed just seemed too big. Amy felt like it was her widow's penance—a vast expanse of emptiness. When Bartlette was in her crib, Amy could roll over three times and not fall off the edge. Or touch another human being.

She turned on the reading lamp. She looked at her youngest. As peaceful now as she was ballistic earlier. Little curls. Incredible soft skin. No lines of tension or worry or defeat on her face. Bartlette was an angel. Even now, she could see that. Bartlette was beautiful. And precious. And gorgeous. And worthy of all the love and all the work and all the patience anyone could muster.

So why ...

Amy stopped on the edge of the precipice. Her eyes filled. She shook her head. She willed herself against the tears. But her heart's momentum could not be stopped.

Why does everything else always go so wrong?

When she felt blue, she was prone to ask questions that were negative statements in disguise. Questions that were really knives that pierced her skin and entered her blood vessels and coursed all around her body, stabbing her with sadness and perplexity.

If that was even a word.

Amy cried for a while.

When the tears slowed and finally stopped, and her eyes felt like they'd been rubbed with 40-grit sandpaper, she reached for the book on her bedside table.

Passionate Marriage: Keeping Love & Intimacy Alive in Committed Relationships.

Excellent.

But Amy had to smile a little. She thought of a sequel. *Keeping Love & Intimacy Alive When Your Husband's Doing Whores.*

Amy had a rule. If you could laugh at yourself, you could not be called pathetic.

She decided to go with it. She shut her eyes and opened the book at a random place—near the back because she reckoned the author usually saved his or her best insights for the conclusion.

She opened her eyes. There it was. The index. From "facial, displays during sex" to "intimacy, other-validated." Oh dear. She repeated the procedure. This time, better luck. She read:

Loss is inherent in getting what you want—unless you want everything, which guarantees you'll be unhappy.

Amy pulled a tissue from a box on the floor and blew her nose. Quietly. Then she grabbed another tissue and blew again.

She shook her head. She didn't want everything. And if loss was part of getting what she wanted, she was well on her way.

Amy shook her head again.

Then she caught herself. She forced herself to nod. Like she had before. When she had the insight about being free, about choosing. But now it just felt weird, stilted. So Amy compromised. She shrugged. Then she leaned down and ever so gently picked up her daughter. She carried Bartlette to the room she shared with Carmen and laid her youngest down to sleep in her crib.

L

Sometimes God smiles. The clouds of fate part, and for a moment, sunshine pours through, sweet and warm and golden.

He was at the door. Charlie. And she hadn't ordered anything. And he wasn't in his milkman's uniform. Just jeans and a polo shirt. And he was smiling. And, unbelievable luck, she had just finished doing her makeup and hair. No kimono, and no décolletage, but her new-bra breasts stood up as straight as she did.

He looked her in the eyes and waited. She looked down and watched him scrunch up the toes of his right foot. He was wearing Tevas. She stood and waited for him to say something. The traffic noise from the freeway seemed strangely loud.

Then music suddenly started from the stereo. Ferguson, bare-chested and wearing only his underpants, pushed his mother out of the way, and grabbed Charlie's hand. The 3-year-old led Charlie into the living room and started dancing across the floor, which was mined with Lego blocks. Charlie joined in, winking at Amy as he picked up his CD cover.

"I was wondering where I left this," he shouted at her.

She felt something fall several stories down an empty elevator shaft in her heart.

Oh.

Charlie had come back for his CD. That explained it. Simple, really.

And devastating.

She went to the kitchen.

A few minutes later, the music changed to *Hot Salsa Hits #4*. Charlie came into the kitchen and found her spreading Nutella on Wheat Thins. It was her favorite stress food. He grabbed one and ate it. She looked at him as if he had broken a holy fast.

He frowned. "I gotta do something, but I don't know how," he said. "What's your excuse?"

He took another Wheat Thin as soon as she had spread it. She smiled compassionately.

"I was stupid enough to think you came to see me," she said. "Now I see you just wanted your music back." She pointed to the CD in his other hand.

"Wrong." He stuffed the choco-cracker in his mouth and slowly opened the CD case. He took the CD out, held it in both his hands for a moment, and then snapped it in half.

Then he walked out of her house without so much as leaving a phone number.

Amy followed him. Outside on the sidewalk, with her makeup done just right and her boobs perky as the morning sunshine, she waved to him in the rear-view mirror of the pizza delivery car he drove.

It advertised MIKE'S MEGA PIZZAS—WHEN YOUR APPETITE'S BIGGER THAN AFRICA. The telephone number to order was 246–8888.

M

IT WAS a form of delaying the inevitable—which, she realized, was the story of life. However.

Besides, she was mothering at the moment. Building towers of plastic cups so Bartlette could destroy them; being an appreciative art critic for Carmen's Q-tip water-color people-scapes (where the people dwarfed their environment); and applauding the winners of Ferguson's Hot Wheels car races.

And she was enjoying every minute of it. Procrastinating, that is. Oh, playing with the kids was all right. But the procrastination was downright luscious.

You see, until she confirmed otherwise, Charlie, Mr. Tan-Supple-Sensitive-Good-with-Kids-Exotic-Dancer-Choreographer, actually may have come to her house just to see her—because she had something to give beside mother's milk and a mother's love. It made her eyes misty just to think that she might be seen as attractive or valued or (complete fantasy) liked for herself.

Her mother would have told her she was being pathetic over a man—over her fantasy of a man. Just knowing her mom would disapprove was all the encouragement she needed to procrastinate a little longer.

Amy knew she could ring the pizza place any time to track Charlie down—even to draw him back by ordering a pizza. But she didn't.

Instead, Amy rang U and explained that a 10-out-of-10 spunk had destroyed something he cared about just to make a point to her. U thought Charlie might just have been tired of the CD, or maybe Ferguson had scratched it. But Amy laughed it off. U's conjecture was even less informed than her own.

The truth was, U didn't know. Only Charlie knew. And he wasn't telling yet. And so, in the land of I-don't-know, Amy pleasured herself with possibilities and the utterly ridiculous, though not yet discounted, idea that Charlie liked her.

Ah, that was one for the Dalai Lama. In the story of life, happiness was achievable, but only while you delayed the inescapably unhappy ending.

Just then, there was a knock at the door. Actually, a number of knocks. Like this: KNOCK-knock-knock, KNOCK-knock-knock.

It was a visitor with a samba beat.

Carmen ran and opened the door. She was immediate awestruck by the sight of two mega pizzas—one Hawaiian and one Bavarian (it had crust like a giant soft pretzel and was topped with sliced *weißwurst* and sauerkraut). Carrying the pizzas was a man wearing a black mask around his eyes and a black skin-tight body suit. The only thing he appeared to have on underneath was a G-string, which the tightness of the material betrayed in relief.

Amy imagined the G-string to be black satin, but immediate verification was impossible.

She invited the masked pizza man into the house. The pizza and its wonderful aroma came with him.

N

SHE knew it was too good to be true: free pizza and a man with buttocks so smooth and ripe under Lycra they looked like they were shaped by Michelangelo.

Charlie said he had to go. He said he had a gig, and he had brought the pizza just to make up for the fact that he left so quickly earlier.

He turned to go. She made a face. "Let me understand this. You're leaving quickly now to make up for leaving quickly before."

"I didn't want to eat and run."

"No," she said. "Just run."

He smiled. "I don't run in costume. It's a little bouncy if you know what I mean."

He kissed her on the forehead and turned to go.

She grabbed him by the wrist.

"Why," she said and stepped outside, closing the front door behind her. "Why pizza? Why visit the independent mom dressed as Zorro and be so nice?"

"Do you think I'm nice?"

"Why, Charlie?" She still held his forearm. Tight. The interrogation, to be effective, had to be carried out at close quarters. She could hardly believe she was passing up a chance to delay the inevitable delivery of bad news. However. She noticed him looking at her hair—the lazy-8 layers, the woof and weave, the luxuriant thickness.

"Charlie?"

"You're kids are inside. Shouldn't you check on them?"

"They won't starve, Charlie. You've seen to that… I guess I should say thank you."

Suddenly, she felt foolish and over-bearing. She dropped his arm and stepped back. "I'm sorry," she said. "I just don't know what's happening."

"I don't know either," he said.

He smiled like an angel and then walked like a devil to the pizza van. She followed.

"What is it that you don't know?"

He looked suddenly sad—as if a cloud passed over his interior sun.

"Besides everything?" He tried to smile again, but it withered. "Well how's this?—I don't know my kid's first name."

Then he got in his van and drove away.

Amy felt rooted to the spot. A minute passed as she stared into space. Then she changed focus and stared at the ground for a while. There was a nickel there. Shiny in the grass. She put it in her pocket and then began staring at the ground again.

Finally, the front door opened, and Carmen asked Amy if she would like to come in so she could eat the ham pieces that Carmen didn't like.

Once inside, it turned out there was more than ham for her. Ferguson was saving the sauerkraut from his Bavarian pizza. He said the smell of it made him feel sick. Bartlette hadn't saved anything, but then she hadn't eaten anything either. She saw the pizza as more of a cadaver than a meal—and had been performing dissections on it ever since it arrived.

Amy picked up her plate heaped with ham and sauerkraut. Then she sat down on the sofa and concentrated. On what she didn't know.

The breadth and the depth of her lack of knowledge was impressive.

However.

O

OPRAH said it, and it was true:

What I know for sure is that there is no strength without challenge, adversity, resistance, and often pain.

Equally true was this thought of Amy's:

What I know for sure is that there is no suffering without challenge, adversity, resistance, and often pain.

The moral was obvious. The difference between strength and suffering was attitude. PDP. Perception. Direction. Persistence. Amy knew from public relations theory that reality was the most malleable concept on the face of the earth. Amy also knew, and so did people everywhere, that what you believe alters what you experience, which eventually alters what is. Example: people with a spiritual faith, any faith, recover from illness better than non-believers.

Nothing to do with religion. Everything to do with individual faith—and faith, as it's applied to everyday existence, is just another word for attitude.

Win one for the Gipper. Send a man to the moon. Find a cure for cancer.

Life might seem like an immovable object. But inside us dwelled an irresistible force. Now, Amy just had to get Charlie's in gear.

This was the story—he told her last night over the phone. He'd had an affair with an Italian woman. ("Not as pretty as you, Amy," he said. Amy felt she liked the woman already.) Her name was Caterina. She was studying English at Cal State Fullerton. They had a week-long "relationship." They were just friends at first, he said, but she had these big, beautiful brown eyes. One night, they started slow-dancing when he was wearing only a pair of tights, and well, you know. (Amy took a mental note of this as a potential route of seduction.) Caterina left for Florence soon afterwards and neither of them was heartbroken. Just one of those flings. But then, a month later, she rang to say she was pregnant. She said she wanted to have the child. He said he thought they should marry. She wasn't so sure and asked him to fly out to talk it over. Unfortunately, he didn't have the money for the flight right away. Two months passed by the time he saved the cash, and when Charlie tried to ring her to arrange the trip, he found her line had been disconnected. That was three years ago. Now Charlie woke up every day feeling guilty. He was missing his kid's childhood. He didn't even know whether it was a boy or a girl. How bad was that?

It was a sad story. But Charlie was stuck in the muck of self-centered suffering. Amy told him so.

Amy knew all about self-suffering. The vicious cycle: self-doubt, self-blame, self-pity. Then the law of emotional inertia kicks in. A person who is depressed tends to stay depressed. Lack of hope tends to destroy any plans to create new hope.

As a fellow sufferer, she of course felt compassion for Charlie's difficulties. She knew what it felt like when life was so tough that the "too-hard" basket was overflowing. But curiously, she wasn't restricted by her own limitations when she thought about Charlie's life. Instead, she felt inspired to help him.

There was, of course, a solution. And, as in any other public relations problem, there were four steps to success.

First, accurately assess the situation. (Where was his child? Where was Caterina? How were they coping? How did Caterina feel about having him enter the child's life at this date?)

Second, decide on his goal. (Did he want to live near the kid? Did he want the kid to live near him? Would visiting every year be enough?)

Third, devise a strategy to deliver the goal desired. (Find out Caterina's phone number and start asking questions.)

Fourth, and most important, believe your own PR. (In a word, attitude. If he wanted to have contact with his child, then that was enough. All he had to do was to try, and keep trying, and eventually he would find a way.)

Amy told Charlie the four points over the phone.

There was a silence. An awkward one, long enough that she noticed the subtle static on the cordless. Then he finally told her he hadn't thought she was the bossy type and said goodbye.

Amy hung up her phone and shrugged.

It was a setback. But it didn't worry her. She felt a seriously positive mental attitude forming in her head.

P

NEVER feed plums and chocolate-covered coffee beans to a seven-month-old baby.

The result, Amy was learning, is explosive.

Amy had been on the phone putting out fires. U was upset because she felt that Amy's new-found positivity, together with her budding whatever-it-was with Charlie, left U little room to "be there" for Amy at this crucial time. In other words, U felt like Amy was shutting her out just when she should be accepting her help.

Amy's mother, Grace, meanwhile, had finally got around to reading the title of the book Amy had given her. Grace was offended. Did Amy think she was a bad mother? Did Amy think she didn't listen? Was Amy saying that for 26 years her mother had got it all wrong? Was that Amy's way of saying thank you?

While Amy was distracted, Carmen decided to play mother and feed baby Bartlette some lunch.

Carmen chose plums because they were yummy. And she chose chocolates—she didn't know they had coffee beans inside—because she could reach them. Amy felt guilty for not putting them away. Still, Bartlette hadn't choked on them. And in spite of her dark sloppy poops, she was as chirpy as a box of birds, pleasantly wired on her first caffeine high.

Fortunately, it was a slow day on the Charlie front. Amy had adopted a maddening indifference approach. By not calling him, she would naturally increase his interest in her, and in any help she might offer in his quest to find his child. Her apparent lack of interest would spark him into action. Absence would make the heart grow more curious, if not fonder. All she had to do was wait.

In the meantime, Amy read more of the book by her friend the Dalai Lama.

Not surprisingly, she discovered that he also believed in the value of personal PR. The Dalai Lama had his own version of attitude adjustment therapy:

> *First learn about the positive value of the practices, then build up determination, and then try to implement them. At the beginning, the implementation of the positive practices is very small, so the negative influences are still very powerful. However, eventually, as you gradually build up the positive practices, the negative behaviors are automatically diminished.*

As you build up the positive, the negative is automatically zapped.

That was a cool idea.

That was a strong attitude.

Bartlette's bottom sounded again. Amy winced and even Ferguson ran away from the smell. Amy lifted her daughter up and saw the poop had escaped the diaper. Blowout.

Another day, Amy's patience would have snapped. But today, the irritation came and went. She let loose a long sigh and felt surprisingly calm.

"Let's clean you up, little girl," she said. And she did.

Q

THE doorbell rang when Amy thought it would. About a day and a half had passed since she last talked to Charlie on the phone. She had just finished feeding her little pumpkins their favorite dinner of penny eggs (eggs scrambled with "pennies" of sliced hot dog) and toast "cookies" (where the kids got to cut their toast into cookie-cutter shapes.)

Ferguson was about to bite into his white-toast gingerbread man when the doorbell rang. "Charlie!" he said. But before he could climb down from his chair, one look from Amy told him he was not allowed to move. Amy wanted to make the first impression alone.

She wore the kimono and the new bra. Hair and makeup were both 9 out of 10. She had even lost 1.6 pounds in the last 36 hours—the Nutella jar had been left untouched, and a virgin box of Wheat Thins had yet to lose its maidenhead. Which was as much an indication of her improved mood as anything.

So it was with confidence that she swung open the front door.

However.

Her spirits fell and went splat like sopping wet towel dropped from a great height. She saw Ed, the real estate salesman, and two strangers standing in front of her.

"Amy, so good to see you," said Ed. He leaned in to kiss her, but she stepped back, leaving him puckering in mid-air. "Let me introduce Quentin and Pearl."

Quentin, a pre-maturely balding 30-something guy, stared at his comfortable yet stylish shoes. Pearl, who had been tilting her head to glimpse inside the house, straightened and offered an insincere smile. She wore narrow, oblong, pointy sunglasses. She peered over them at Amy's breasts and then tilted to Amy's face. Pearl was short.

Amy crossed her arms. She said nothing.

"I wanted to call," explained Ed, offering his hand, which Amy didn't take. "But Quentin and Pearl insisted."

"He insisted," said Pearl, indicating the fork-tongued Ed. "He said you were desperate to sell."

"Desperate in a very patient way," said Ed. "I mean, like all good sellers, you're motivated. But I know you won't consider an offer that's not market-worthy. Absolutely market-worthy. That's why Quentin and Pearl are here."

There was a silence. Pearl said something under her voice and retreated a few steps to make a cellphone call. Quentin held his ground, showing his bald pate to Amy as he continued to stare at his shoes. Their black leather glowed in the late afternoon light with a muted, buttery luster.

"So," said Ed, "would it inconvenience you too much if we had a quick look around the place? Don't worry. You don't have to clean up. Quentin and Pearl like to see a place lived-in."

Amy gestured for them both to back up. Then she reached down and picked up the mat just beyond the threshold. It had "Welcome" painted on it in faded letters. She flipped it over in one motion. A cloud of dust rose. When it settled, Ed, Pearl and Quentin read the far brighter message on the obverse.

Quentin, whose point of view was ideally placed to appreciate the message, burst out laughing.

It said: F*** OFF. It was one of those stupid things that Bart used to bring back from his road trips. At the time he gave it to Amy, she thought it was another example of his incredibly bad taste. Now, she realized even Bart had a clue sometimes.

Ed finally got the hint. "Maybe another time? Quentin and Pearl are very serious buyers. And I don't think they mind me telling you, their finance is already pre-approved."

Amy's arms crossed on her chest again. Pearl huffed and puffed and said she was going. But Quentin looked up from his shoes and straight into Amy's eyes. "I think I have to make the holes for the shoelaces a bit bigger," he said.

She couldn't help smiling.

"He's a shoemaker," said Ed. He whispered loudly as if Quentin wasn't there. "Designs shoes for the Hollywood stars. Organic leather. Handmade. A thousand bucks each." Ed laughed. "Each shoe, that is. Can you believe it?"

Quentin smiled. "They're great shoes." He spoke to Amy, who noticed he had very kind brown eyes. "I do a plaster cast of each foot. Then I design the shoe together with a reflexologist, so you get a foot massage while you walk. I call them Qools. With a Q."

Ed saw that Amy's arms were no longer crossed and she was listening. "So maybe we could have a look now. Just five minutes."

However, Quentin was already walking away in his great shoes. "C'mon, Ed," he said over his shoulder. "She's expecting company. And it aint us."

Amy stood and watched as Ed opened car doors for Pearl and Quentin. Ed was about to slip into the driver's seat when he stopped, pulled out a business card from his pocket, scribbled something on the back, and stuck it in Amy's mailbox.

Amy closed the front door and discovered all three of her children were waiting for her in the living room. Carmen was holding Bartlette.

Ferguson said, "What does the doormat say?"

"Could that man make some shoes for me?" said Carmen. "I want a foot message when I walk, too. They could be princess shoes."

Baby Bartlette just gurgled and cooed.

R

THE maddening indifference approach has only one drawback—it usually doesn't work. Three days had passed, and Charlie had not so much as delivered a pizza. However.

There was a Plan B.

Solicitation. Of a nonsexual nature. To be followed by groveling, if necessary. Also, of a nonsexual nature. To be followed by mutual attraction and passion. Quite possibility of a sexual nature. However.

Decisions about sex should not be made unilaterally or in advance.

Passion was a face-to-face, moment-to-moment thing. The planning served only to create the opportunity for romance. Love, though it might be encouraged, could not be manufactured.

Amy stopped for a moment. The phone was in her hand, and she was poised to dial. She felt a thrill run through her body. She liked this. This seeking a relationship. This being the pursuer. This role that men got to take most of the time. It was as if she had control. Clearly, she didn't. But she was the one calling, she was the one trying to make things happen, she was the one being clear about her attraction to an appealing male of the same species. No passivity. Only positivity.

God, she was disgustingly upbeat lately.

Charlie answered at the pizza number. He laughed when he heard her voice.

"What?" she said.

"I knew you'd call," he said.

"What are you talking about?"

"If I waited long enough." He laughed again. Not a mean laugh, but annoyingly superior just the same.

She'd been out-indifferenced. And it was definitely maddening.

She said nothing and waited for a whole minute with the phone pivoted away from her mouth so he couldn't even hear her breathing.

"Look, Amy," he said at last, capitulating in Round Two of the waiting game. "I'm glad you called. I wanted to tell you that my big freak-out is over. I got Caterina's number on the Internet, and I talked to her this morning. It's all OK."

"What's OK? Your child?"

"No." Charlie's voice went low. She imagined him closing his eyes the way he did when he felt self-conscious. "There isn't a kid. Not one that's alive, anyway."

Amy responded by waiting.

"Caterina said she miscarried." Charlie took a breath. Explaining the details of such a private story while standing in a takeout pizza kitchen was probably weird and awkward. Charlie carried on anyway. "It was pretty early. Second month, she said. She didn't want to tell me back then. It was too hard. Then she moved house."

"She could be lying." Amy spoke before she thought. She felt angry—though she wasn't sure why.

Charlie laughed. "I don't think so. She invited me out to Rome, that's where she lives now. She runs a nightclub there. She wanted me to be a dancer." He laughed again. In a sad way.

"Why are you laughing?"

"It's just that life's bizarre. I wanted to find out about my kid. But it turns out she never was born. I get an offer to work as a dancer. But I turn it down."

There was another silence. "Wouldn't she let you choreograph?"

"Choreography," he said. His voice was suddenly flat. "Yeah, she didn't really care what I did on stage. She was more interested in how I performed between shows. Horizontal choreography, yeah, she would have given me creative control on that."

Another silence transpired. Amy could hear an impatient voice in the background and the hustle and bustle of the pizza kitchen.

"You're nice," he said.

"Thanks. Is that good or bad?"

"Good," he said. "Definitely. In x-ray we used to say it's all about the contrast. The clarity of an image depends on it. You see the negative and the positive juxtaposed. You know?"

She didn't know what he was getting at. In fact, just then, she felt lost at sea. No ship, no compass, only a life jacket that somehow came from her heart and enveloped her chest, making her entire body buoyant—directionless and lost, but buoyant.

Was he saying she was too nice to fall for? Not sexy enough? Did he think she would judge him for being offered a job as a part-time hooker?

"You're nice, too," she said.

"That's not the point. I've seen you with your kids. You're a great mom. Sometimes, I just watch you out of the corner of my eye—how you pay attention to each of them, how you listen and love them even though you're tired. That's nice. That's good. I don't think Caterina would have done that."

Amy had just received more appreciation in 30 seconds of conversation with Charlie than she'd had in four years of marriage with Bart.

Charlie kept on talking. "Me, I'm just feeling sad now. About my kid. My might-have-been kid. My might-have-been fatherhood. I was worried about it, but I guess I was excited, too." He laughed his sad laugh.

Amy shook her head on the phone. She was trying to maintain some equilibrium, but she felt herself getting choked up.

"I bought her a present last week, you know. Pretty stupid. Those plastic cups that all fit into each other or you can stack them in a tower. And they're in different colors. When I bought the cups, I thought, 'Wow, it must be cool to teach your kid about that.' I mean, blue is the color of the sky and the ocean. The color of a candle flame at the bottom. I always liked that blue. I decided I wanted to teach my kid about that color. I wanted to show her that."

Charlie stopped talking. She didn't say anything.

"Those cups, they're good for pouring games, too. Kids like playing with water, you know."

"I know," she said. "Those cups are great."

S

Amy didn't know what to do.

"I think I'm in like," she whispered over the plastic lid of her paper-cup Americano. "At first I thought it was just lust, then I thought it might be that I wanted to prove something to myself, but now I think I really like him."

"OK, don't panic," said U. "Stay calm." She stood up and started walking back and forth in the smallish kitchen, holding her coffee in two hands in front of her like a ceremonial urn. Her hair was in pigtails. She wore her WHY ME? t-shirt.

"You're pacing," said Amy.

U stopped and looked hard at Amy. "I'm the one who has to handle all the stress of keeping you relaxed." U finally swung into a chair—first spinning it so it was back to front, like cowboys used to do in the movies.

Ferguson noticed this and was impressed. He tried to copy it with his kid-size plastic chair. Carmen sat across from him at their kid-size table devouring Nutella on Wheat Thins and on slices of apple.

Bartlette emitted a low-level but steady whine from her mother's arms. She had sprouted a tooth, and along with it, a temperature and a rash on her bottom.

U took hold of Amy's hand. Amy noticed her friend's fingers were trembling.

"How many lattes today, U?"

"Seven," she smiled and drank deeply from her cup. "But every other one I order half-strength."

"I think County Hospital runs an exchange program. If you turn in your coffee beans, they give you decaf in a clean cup."

"You're changing the subject."

"Avoidance behavior is the only way I can calm down enough to face the problems of my life," said Amy.

"You're just scared. Admit it."

"What are you scared of, Mommy?" asked Carmen.

"Nothing, dear. I'm fearless."

"What's fearless?" said Ferguson.

"It's where you pretend not to be scared," said U.

"I can do that," said Carmen.

Everyone laughed. Then U leaned over and whispered to Amy, "OK, here's the litmus test for being 'in like.' Ready? Close your eyes and imagine your favorite hunk—Brad Pitt, Cary Grant, whoever."

"OK."

"Who is it?"

"I'm not telling."

"You are so boring sometimes."

"Mysterious."

"Anyway. Now imagine you have call waiting."

"Can I have really fast Internet, too?"

"Stop fooling around. OK, you've got Brad or Cary on the line and the guy is hot for you, whispering how he's completely infatuated and asking you out to some fantastic place to eat—and then, just then, you get a call from Charlie. Do you tell Brad to wait, and take Charlie's call? What do you do?"

"You're weird," whispered Amy.

"This is important," said U.

"What's important?" said Carmen, whose hearing had improved markedly now that she wasn't chomping on Wheat Thins.

"Nothing," said U.

"Everything," said Amy.

Carmen shook her head. "Why are you whispering?"

"To save our voices," said U.

"So we can talk longer," said Amy. "Friends do that sometimes."

Bartlette let out a howl. Amy stood up to give her a few soothing knee bends.

"Don't try to escape this," said U. "Close your eyes again. Can you imagine it?"

"Yeah, OK," said Amy, shutting her eyes and smiling. But the smile vanished as the seconds ticked by. Frown lines appeared on her face.

"OK, fine," whispered U in her ear. "Now you ask yourself the question. With that complete situation surrounding you—experiencing what you feel there—go ahead and ask yourself the question."

There was a pause. Amy stopped doing her knee bends. She peeked out at U. "What's the question again?"

"Who do you put on hold? Jesus, Amy, this is your life we're talking about."

Suddenly, there was a big bang and Ferguson, who had been working on the cowboy backwards-chair-sit-down method, went down on his elbow. It smarted. Tears appeared in his eyes, but he jumped up. He grabbed his chair and shook it in anger. Then he started to try the move again, but stopped. He took a breath and closed his eyes. He stood still there for quite a long time.

At last Amy asked, "Fergie, honey. What are you doing?"

He opened one eye. "I'm doing 'fearless.' You know, pretending. But it takes a long time because my elbow hurts."

Amy bent over and kissed him on his head. "I know, honey. You take your time."

When she straightened, U confronted her. "Well?" she whispered. "Did you take his call?"

Carmen drew close, sensing that important information was about to be shared.

Amy just smiled and nodded. It was a huge grin of a smile, too. But U knew there was more to it than that. "Why were you frowning before?"

"Denzel said he'd wait for me forever if he had to. He wanted me that much. It made it a tough decision."

U sighed long and deep and then left to get more coffee.

Amy caught her at the front door. For the first time that afternoon, Amy looked worried. "What do I do now?"

It was U's turn to smile. "Order pizza," she said.

T

THE diamond wasn't anything amazing. That's what made it so painful.

In fact, the stone was so small it could hardly be distinguished from its silver setting. No dramatic glints of light played off its facets; there were no flashes of iridescent color. It wasn't ugly, but it wasn't dazzling either. In fact, to be blunt, it was on the tacky side of inexpensive.

But perhaps that's just what a career-transitioning guy like Charlie would choose.

Amy tried to shove her heart into reverse.

Amy remembered the rock that Bart had bought for her. To him, it was a symbol of his ability to provide, a symbol of his net worth. To Charlie, the cheap ring would mean something very different—a sacrifice in the name of love. A symbol of his ability to transcend his own cash-flow problems to honor the woman he adored.

It was romantic. Even moving. The problem was the ring sat on Danielle's finger. The fake blonde delivery chick with the railroad spike in her navel. And Danielle was now working for Mike's Mega Pizzas, standing behind the counter instead of Charlie.

At great personal cost, Amy had convinced her mother to babysit again so she could go and see Charlie. Mother had demanded a night on the town just the two of them—so they (she) could talk. Amy had agreed.

Now Amy was staring at Danielle's ring. Danielle frowned and popped a piece of Trident sugarless gum in her mouth. "It's busy today. Do you know what you want?"

"Charlie," said Amy.

"Not here today. I'll take your order."

"Where is he?"

"Who are you?"

"Amy Franklin." She paused. "Amy Dellaconta Franklin."

"Oh, yeah," said Danielle. "I remember. The ice cream lady with the rude kid."

Amy wanted to get angry, but instead she just felt rattled.

"Can you just tell me if he's coming in to work later?"

Danielle shook her head. "Look, uh, Amy, don't you think you're a little old for him?" She laughed. "Anyway, it's too late." She waved her ringed hand in the air. "I noticed you noticing."

Amy steeled herself to reply, but found she could say nothing.

"Get real," said Danielle. "Charlie and I are getting married. So why don't you find some other pizza place to pick up men, OK?"

Danielle turned her back to attend to one of the pizza ovens, showing her tight buns in hip-hugging workout shorts to Amy. Amy did not move.

After a minute, Danielle turned back. Sweat beaded on her brow from the ovens. She unzipped her sweatshirt to reveal sculpted cleavage. She made a face at Amy to show her impatience.

"Are you a stalker or something? Do I have to call the police?"

Amy waited a few seconds. Then she beckoned Danielle forward and lowered her voice. "Breasts," she said. "Asymmetrical.... If I were you, I'd demand my money back."

Danielle reflexively looked down and zipped up her sweatshirt.

By the time she looked up, Amy was gone.

U

Ferguson had a hard poo. He grunted on the toilet like a baby mastodon. Unnh! Unnh! The poo wouldn't come out, and so his grunts grew more impassioned. And desperate. Uuuuunnh! No go. At last, he cried out to his mother.

But he didn't need to. He'd left the door to the bathroom open, and Amy had been following the sonic progression of the bowel movement as she changed the dirty diaper of her youngest.

"Mom!" he yelled.

She pulled up Bartlette's pants, hoisted her to a hip and headed for the kitchen.

"Uuuuuunnnh!" Ferguson gave it one more try and collapsed, burying his head in his legs. "Mom!" he yelled into the space between his knees. "Mom, my bottom is stuck up!"

"Lower your voice," she said. "It's bad manners to yell while you're pooping."

Ferguson looked up. Amy had already arrived in the bathroom. She handed him a tall plastic tumbler of water. "Drink this."

His eyebrows rose and his eyes filled with a mixture of confusion and wonder.

"Drink it now. Then pull up your pants and go play. Your bottom will tell you when it's ready."

Ferguson drank the water in quick sips and did what his mother said. She looked like she might get mad and he didn't want to chance it. He left, and she closed the door behind him.

She closed the lid on the toilet and sat down, putting Bartlette on the not-exactly-pristine bathroom floor to play. That in itself was an indication of her mental state. In short, she felt like screaming. Losing someone you like isn't the end of the world. She knew that in her head. But in her heart, her recently brave heart, it felt like she'd been cut to the quick, and it made it far worse that she'd lost Charlie to a woman like Danielle.

Time passed. Bartlette pulled all the toilet paper off the roll. Amy watched her do it without lifting a finger, only dumping the soft, looping coils of TP in the bathtub when it became apparent that Bartlette wanted to eat her handiwork. Amy then picked up her daughter and breast-fed her till she slept. But Amy didn't leave the bathroom or the toilet seat. She just sat and sat. Until there was a knock at the door.

Amy opened it, still holding the sleeping Bartlette.

Ferguson stood there holding out a tumbler of water.

"Drink it now," he said and glanced behind him.

"There's a man."

V

QUENTIN, the bald shoemaker, stood in the front doorway.

She asked him how long he'd been waiting.

"About 15 minutes," he said.

"Oh dear," she said.

He told her not to worry. He said he wanted to ask Amy a question, though he realized it might not be the right time—especially if, as her son had explained, she was having hard poos.

Amy looked down at the tumbler she held, blushing a little. "You know kids," she said, "if they're feeling one way then the whole world must be."

"I am, therefore you are too," he said.

They both smiled. And that's when their eyes met. It was unexpected and hard to believe, but for a moment, she felt both understood and understanding. For a moment, though they didn't know each other at all, they seemed to inhabit a quiet, transparent bubble of amiable compassion.

It was, of course, a shock to the system. She looked down at her baby to break the spell. Then she realized she must be mistaken. This man had no reason to be at her door. She didn't know him except as an unexpected and unwanted prospective house buyer. She closed the door to an opening of 6 inches. She told him this was a bad time. Then she started shutting the door completely.

"Eustazia said it would be okay," he said. She stopped the door at 3 inches. "She temps for me, U does. Customer service. She says service, no matter how self-sacrificial, is her middle name."

Amy laughed in spite of her suspicions. Clearly, he knew U.

Quentin leaned toward the open gap at the threshold, quickly adding that he had dropped by to see if she wanted him to make casts of her feet. For a pair of Qools. Then he stepped back, disappearing from view.

She opened the door wider.

He looked down and shuffled the exquisite shoes he wore, admiring them as he did.

She said she couldn't afford a pair of his shoes, though it was nice of him to ask.

At that point, Ferguson, who was trying to be a good host while encouraging regularity, ran in with another plastic tumbler of water. It was meant for Quentin, and when Ferguson tripped, Quentin got it—all over his pants leg, a leather carry bag he held, and his incredibly expensive shoes.

Ferguson looked up in doubt and fear. But Quentin was smiling. He helped Ferguson up. "Do you have a towel, young man?" Fergie turned to Amy for guidance. She nodded. So he took Quentin back to the bathroom to get dry. Amy followed.

Quentin laughed when he saw the bathtub and what Bartlette had done. "How cool," he said. "Taking a bath in toilet paper. Was that your idea or the kid's?"

"Mine," she said. "You being sarcastic?"

He wasn't. He caught her eye again. "The advantages are obvious. You don't get wet, so you don't have to dry off."

'No puddles on the floor,' she said.

"And if you need to cry," he turned and bent down to tear off a hunk of TP, "you're more than prepared."

Back in the living room, he explained that the shoes were free for her because he had an experimental design he wanted to try out, and she would be a guinea pig. The shoes might not be comfortable at all, he said. They might be a cobbling catastrophe. Would she consent to letting him take a mold? Would she take the risk that the shoes might be a failure? What did she think?

She felt doubts arise in her mind. Another strange man in her house. And this one had a strange request. Then she realized that the mind is where doubts breed. Happiness, on the other hand, got fruitful and multiplied in the heart. The heart was where positive practices made their magic happen, where wisdom lay. Wow, she thought to herself. Thank you, Dalai Lama.

A smile slowly dawned on her face. He smiled back. Neither said a word. Neither lowered their gaze.

"You have presence," he said at last.

She winked at him. "And you have a mold to make," she said. Then she led him to the kitchen. "You okay working in here?"

From his bag, he removed a white drop cloth, the petroleum jelly (for coating the skin to make the cast removable), the plaster of Paris strips and pair of funny scissors. Then he started soaking the plaster strips in a bowl before layering them on

Amy's feet. The kids watched, fascinated, as Quentin sculpted the wet white strips around her foot. When he was done, he asked the kids if they wanted to make casts of their feet, too. Just for fun. Of course, they said yes. So did Amy.

It was the kids' bedtime before Quentin and Amy could finish their conversation. So he waited while she tucked them in, and when she returned, he had somehow managed to set her kitchen table with a pressed white linen tablecloth. A loaf of Vior's sourdough bread lay sliced on a cutting board, surrounded by Brie, Camembert, fresh mozzarella, black olives, a bottle of red wine and two elegant wineglasses. Candle flames danced languidly on top of white tapers.

She was flabbergasted and strangely moved. But before she said a word, it all dawned on her—free shoes, nice to the kids, fancy food. Her hands landed on her hips, elbows pointed out in defiance, and she tilted her head to an appropriately skeptical angle.

"The house isn't for sale," she said with a frown.

He laughed. "I'm not interested in buying a house. Pearl is."

She began to object, but he cut her off.

"Business partners. She does the books, admin, marketing and that stuff." He shrugged. "I just came along for a second opinion. Or that's what I told her. Actually…" He smiled and his eyes sparkled. "Actually, Eddie told me he knew this widow who was a total babe."

She raised one eyebrow.

"Anyway," he continued. "Tonight I brought a little something to eat and drink in case you were hungry. Then I left it in the car because I was nervous. I imagined you might think it was a bit forward to arrive with a picnic. But when you tucked the kids in, I had a re-think and decided that being forward was the only way to avoid going backward. So… surprise! I hope you don't mind."

She picked up the bottle and poured two glasses.

"You are so full of shit, Quentin."

"Sometimes," he said. "But only with the best intentions." He held up his glass, and they drank together.

W

Wine, cheese, olives, more wine. They talked. He listened. She felt tipsy. She knew she was really enjoying herself, enjoying being herself. Laughing. Just laughing. And now, somehow, Quentin was kneeling before her and rubbing her feet with rose-scented oil. Her toes, her insoles, her Achilles tendons. Her eyes shut with the pleasure of it, with the touch of his strong, gentle hands.

Naturally, it felt wrong.

However.

She delayed the end of gratification as long as she could. Then she spoke.

"This is wrong," she said.

He stopped rubbing. She opened her eyes. He nodded and moved her warm, pleasured feet to an empty chair.

Amy told her story. She explained how she had finally fallen seriously in like, had finally mustered the gumption to pursue it, and then discovered her beliked was already betrothed. To a hard-bodied, pudding-brained wastrel of a woman.

"Bad timing," she said.

"Maybe," he said. Then he told her the story of his favorite movie. *City of Angels.*

Nicholas Cage was an angel who fell in love with a human played by Meg Ryan. She loved him, too, but freaked out when she found out he was an angel. It was all over between them until he decided he would give up his immortality—and his heavenly status—and become a human. She was overjoyed. They were very happy together for one night and one morning. And then she was killed by a truck while bicycling to get supplies for his breakfast.

"Was she wearing a helmet?"

"Wouldn't have mattered," said Quentin. "Very large truck."

"Not exactly a happy ending," she said.

"That wasn't the ending," he said. "Nicholas Cage buried her and went into a long, very blue funk. After a while, one of his old angel friends appeared to him and asked him a key question. Would he do it again, knowing what he knew now?"

Quentin stopped. He caught Amy's glance and held it. "What do you think he said?"

"Did he love her?"

"He gave up being an angel to be with her."

"So it had to be love."

"Yeah, I think so."

She smiled. "Then the answer's obvious."

"Yeah," said Quentin. "Love is wild."

There was a moment. They drank some more wine. "So what did he say, Nicholas Cage, I mean?"

"He said he would do it again. Even if it was for only one touch of her hair or her skin."

"How did it end?"

"He was bummed for a long time. But at last, he woke up at sunrise one day and went bodysurfing."

"Oh," she said. "What was that supposed to show?"

He paused. "The gate," he said, "is also the gateway."

Then he got up, gathered his plaster casts, his basket of wine glasses and leftover bread and cheese, and said goodnight. He dipped his head and his eyes, then slowly he straightened, and let himself out.

X

True romantic love is like a personalized parking space. You can put any car you want in there, but there's only one name on the asphalt.

The world according to Quentin. Sweet, intuitive, unstressed, even-keeled, quirky, Qool Quentin. He said it over the phone. When he invited her to a "romantic picnic." His words, not her interpretation. However.

Sunset at the beach. It did sound romantic. Revelations of the heart, he said, and the "only thing that feels better on your feet than my shoes."

She said she couldn't get child care. He told her not to worry. The kids were welcome, too. The beach was the biggest playground in the world.

She felt disappointed. And relieved. How could it be romantic with the gang of three munchkin monsters along? But then again, at a time when she wasn't sure of her feelings, it felt much safer to have her offspring with her to act as ballast in the gondola of love.

Now she sat in the reflected glory of the sun as it sank in deepening tones of orange over the smooth Pacific. Quentin poured sand over her toes. And Bartlette's.

Bartlette giggled and squirmed. And kept wanting more sand. Ferguson and Carmen were at the high-tide line building bucket-shaped sandcastles, decorating them with crosses or X's for windows and topping them with flags of seagull feathers and seaweed.

She felt content. It was a glorious moment. A glorious feeling. Things seemed right with the world even though she knew they weren't. But worries had no place here at the beach. Here was peace. Here was comfort.

She decided to take a chance.

"You know that movie you were telling me about," she said. "I think I get what the story is about."

He nodded and continued to pour sand over her toes and her daughter's.

"It's about accepting the loss of love, without getting embittered—keeping your heart open."

He shrugged.

"What?" she said.

"That's not what it's about," he said. "Not the main part, anyway." He continued pouring sand.

She felt a burning sensation come over her face. She felt angry and embarrassed. And suddenly, he seemed not just quiet and calm, but smug, too.

She hit his pouring hand with a plastic spade. He stopped the delicious dribbling of sand over her toes. He looked up and over her head.

"Dinner's here," he said.

Y

Charlie stood in the sunset's orange wash—a heavenly-lit incongruous mix of well-sculpted manhood, cheap costuming and convenience food.

He wore his black Zorro mask, no shirt and black tights. In one hand, he held a large portable stereo. In the other, he balanced an oversized box containing one of Mike's "Mother-of-All" Mega Pizzas—it looked to have the circumference of an open golf umbrella. His stomach muscles rolled and reset themselves as he took an uneasy breath. A frown grew on his face.

"I can't do this," he said. He put down the pizza, pulled a $50 bill from his tights and held it out to Quentin. But Quentin was already moving away, saying over his shoulder, "It'll be fine. It'll be fine. Go ahead. I forgot something in the car." By this time, Ferguson and Carmen had noticed Charlie. They rushed up to welcome him. He smiled at them. And then looked for the first time in the eyes of Amy.

She felt like an army of Argentine ants were moving *en masse* under her skin. She had been the object of no one's desire for so long. Now she just wanted to hide. No, check that. First kill Quentin, then hide.

Ferguson broke the silence by pushing play on the boom box. A sizzling run on a marimba gave way to a sultry merengue beat. Ferguson pulled on Charlie's arm and pleaded. At first Charlie resisted, but then he swept up Ferguson in his arms and performed an impromptu dance while holding the 3-year-old. There were lots of dips and spins and swings, and before long Ferguson was giggling uncontrollably. Carmen jumped forward to dance alongside Charlie. Even baby Bartlette jiggled to the music.

Amy found herself smiling, which led to big beaming smiles from Charlie. When the song ended, Charlie put Ferguson down. "Again, again, again!" said Ferguson.

But three bars into the next song, the music stopped. Eustazia took her finger from the pause button. "Time to go get some frozen yogurt with Aunty U."

Quentin was just behind her. He bowed his head to Amy. "I'm sorry. There's an emergency at the factory. Problem with the waterproofing on the laces of a big export shipment. It's urgent." He looked down at his feet and frowned. He looked up and forced a smile.

"Fortunately, Eustazia has volunteered to look after the kids."

"You told me you were busy," said Amy, staring at U.

"Yeah, I was. Doing this."

Eustazia bent down to whisper to Amy. "He told me you were desperate. So, of course, I dropped everything."

U scooped up Bartlette, and the other kids gathered around her. It was all pretty weird, but the frozen yogurt came with jelly beans on top and that beat pizza any day.

Quentin turned to Charlie but spoke to his feet. "Can you give Amy a ride home?"

Charlie said sure, and the kids and U trooped back across the sand to the parking area. Quentin took charge of the rear guard, being at the moment more of a trudger than a trooper.

It was all a setup, of course. Amy could see that. An elaborate setup. But why would Quentin go to all the trouble? Especially when Charlie was engaged. She found her eyes getting wet. The ants under her skin began another march.

Between Amy and Charlie there wasn't a word. They sat in the twilight and watched the children and the adults get into two cars and drive off.

"Pizza's getting cold." Charlie spoke first.

She nodded. There was silence.

"It's half Mongolian Beef Barbecue and half Thai Tofu."

He held out a gloppy piece. She shook her head. He took a bite.

"What I want to know is why you are marrying Danielle."

The Thai Tofu almost came out his nose. When he recovered, he denied he was marrying anyone. He explained that Danielle had bought the ring for herself because she said guys kept hitting on her at the pizza place. In fact, Danielle didn't even tell Charlie that Amy had come looking for him.

"So there's nothing between you and Danielle?"

"Not anymore," he said. "She was a wrong turn. And you know how one wrong turn can lead to another before you stop being lost."

The ants disappeared. Champagne bubbles took their place.

"So Danielle is full of shit."

"Yup."

"And what am I then?"

"Yourself," he said. It was his complete answer. She waited for elaboration, but Charlie said nothing more. He just put down his pizza and moved closer. The sky was turning to purple, Venus sparked into view above the horizon. Charlie lit one of the long white candles Quentin had brought to the beach. He stuck it in the sand in front of them. Then he moved closer again.

He whispered to her. "I told you before. You're good. And you're for real."

They kissed. Not a single skyrocket screamed into the air. Not a firecracker popped. No fountains of color erupted and fell against the sky. But the feeling in her heart and all through her body was July the 4th.

After a while, when the night had grown chilly and they had grown hot and bothered, she broke away, remembering he had to get back to work. He explained that his shift was over. In fact, his job was over. He had quit.

He sat up, full of excitement.

"I got into a choreography degree program at the University of Utah. I was on the waiting list, but they just called. I have to be there in a week."

"Oh," she said.

They watched the candle flutter in the breeze for a while. She fully understood that on the brink of realizing her romantic fantasy, she now confronted a speeding headlight accelerating toward her in the tunnel of love.

Nonetheless, she tried to be rational. "Utah for exotic dance?"

"Don't you see? It's about learning choreography. All kinds of choreography. I can always get exotic with it later."

She nodded, but inside she was shaking her head and stomping her feet.

He kept talking. "I'm sweet, really. I mean except for not having money for tuition. Or a place to stay. But maybe I can moonlight doing x-rays. Anyway, I figure I just have to believe in my PR like you said and things will work out, right?"

"What about my PR?"

"You can come, too," he said—like he was inviting her to the movies. "Bring the kids." He smiled. A genuine smile for a genuine invitation.

She smiled back, but hers was a cover. Internally, she carried on the conversation. She wasn't irresponsible. She would never risk uprooting the kids to go on what was likely to be a romantic kamikaze mission. No money, no foundation to the relationship, no commitment. Hell, it would even involve moving house, one of the top ten stressors of modern life. She tried to imagine making a home with a guy who changed his jobs more often than he changed his socks.

He was yummy, though. A bronze god. With a good heart. And abs that could crack walnuts. He was a good guy.

He just didn't understand. Not yet anyway. And he was leaving in a week.

Maybe not time enough for love. But what if they had the honeymoon and forgot about the marriage?

She didn't say anything for a long while, looking at the sea and listening to the tide. She closed her eyes and felt the sea breeze against her eyelids. He just held her hand and waited.

Finally, she took his other hand in hers. "Congratulations," she said and kissed him on the cheek.

Then she opened the pizza box. "Which side is Mongolian Beef?"

Z

Charlie wrote every week. She read the letters to the kids. They loved listening to his adventures. He was happy even though his attempts to convince the Mormons that exotic dance could be done to the glory of God had so far proven unsuccessful. He sent CDs of hot Rocky Mountain Latino music for Ferguson.

It was good and genuine and not romantic.

Each letter made Amy feel wistful and regret that her life's lessons dovetailed so closely with self-denial. But she and Charlie had agreed before he left. No strings. Long-distance relationships were too difficult. With his body, long-distance fidelity would be near impossible—even in the land of Moroni.

Initially, he had disagreed. He believed they shouldn't second-guess the future—especially when they hadn't even seen if they were sexually compatible. Every man's relationship litmus test.

For her part, there were times when she was as randy as any man. And she had no doubts about their ability to mutually enjoy each other. That's what worried her. She didn't like the idea of starting something that they couldn't continue. He felt they needed to start to see if they wanted to continue, and then they could make it up as they went. She could see his point. But in the end, it was an intuition thing. She was right. She felt it, and she had to stay true to that.

And she did.

Except for the night before he left for Utah.

But that was his fault. He offered to brush her hair with the stiff-bristled brush, and they ended up in the shower naked together, ostensibly so he could use the coconut-kiwifruit de-tangling conditioner and follicle rejuvenator.

None of the kids woke up once.

It was a mind-altering experience, of course.

Just not mind-changing.

In spite of the spectacular sex, and its intense sweetness coming after all the years in the wilderness, she felt content to say goodbye. And he had his exotic choreography to focus on.

For a while, she wondered why she wasn't heartbroken and missing him madly. It seemed so odd after their courtship and the fantastic night-before farewell. Then after several weeks, she understood.

Her lack of attachment was itself the point. She liked him a lot. But he wasn't a must-have. The point was this: she wasn't desperate.

She wondered about Quentin, what his angle was, why he had done what he did at the beach. But he never called.

He did knock on the door, however.

It was autumn. Blue skies, no smog. Neither cool, nor warm. Charlie had been in Utah for months. She came to the door expecting nothing. Bartlette came with her. She was walking now. And falling. About every third step.

Amy opened the door and found an exquisite pair of butter-smooth mocha leather Qools on the doormat.

Bartlette fell down on them immediately, triggering a mother-daughter wrestling match. Quentin stood five paces away, on the lawn, and chuckled.

Amy held the shoes above the grasp of her daughter and caught the shoemaker's eye.

"I'd say thank you," she said. "But I'm not sure you can hear me at that distance."

He stepped to the side, and behind him in order from smallest to biggest, were a set of Qools for each of her children. Amy felt her heart skip. Ferguson and Carmen by this time had come out to see what was happening. They rushed into the front yard and then descended on the shoes from either side in a pincer movement. Bartlette followed them as fast as she could fall, get back up and fall again.

"They're beautiful," said Amy. She felt her eyes welling with tears. "They're all so beautiful."

The kids were trying the shoes on. Quentin was helping them. Naturally, he had a shoehorn in his pocket.

"If they're not the right size," he told them. "I can adjust them."

He looked up at Amy. "What about yours? Try them."

She swallowed in an effort to gain self-control and stem the tears flooding her eyes. "Sure," she said. "But first, please come in."

She turned to go inside, but he stayed where he was. The children ran around in their own worlds of excitement on the brown grass of the dry lawn. It had been a long time since they had got new shoes from anywhere but the discount footwear outlet.

"Won't you come in?" she said, feeling that familiar sense of impending rejection coming on.

"Maybe," he said. "I mean, it depends." He looked at her with an unwavering gaze. "How long can I stay?"

She didn't answer. The question, coming as it did, and when it did, was a kind of emotional chiropractic adjustment. She felt issues click into place like vertebrae. Zip-zap-zoop. She smiled. Tears now tracked down her cheeks.

Unexpectedly, she had nothing to say. Joy can be like that. But some questions required clear answers. So she put on the posh shoes he had made and walked out to Quentin in Qool comfort.

She stopped a moment and looked down. The shoes did feel like gloves for her feet. Then she looked up, took his face in both her hands and kissed him.

As Ferguson would relate for days and months and years to come, it was right on the lips and right in front of everyone.

LATER, over coffee, he told her what he thought the movie with Nicholas Cage was really about.

"Choosing love," he said. "No matter the cost. In spite of the doubts and the dangers. Because, if you don't, you deny yourself."

"But you set me up with Charlie at the beach," Amy said.

"Part of my plan. You needed to taste that apple."

"Risky plan," said Amy. "That apple tasted really good, you know."

"And you could have chosen to stay with that apple," Quentin replied. Then he shrugged like he was shaking a leaf from a shoulder. "My point is—who are you having coffee with right now?"

She squeezed his hand. The one she'd been holding across the table throughout the entire conversation.

"You're very confident of yourself, aren't you?"

"No," he said. "Just the opposite."

Bartlette wandered up, climbed into Amy's lap and lifted her shirt. She started nursing her daughter without even thinking about it. Quentin smiled.

"I am," he said, "very confident about you, however."

"However," she answered and raised an eyebrow. Then she leaned towards him to collect the kiss he was already in the process of delivering.

2007

Epilogue

It was the Friday afternoon before Mother's Day. Almost home time. Amy stood in front of her middle school class, explaining how jokes depend on double meanings. Then she stopped in mid-sentence.

A familiar young girl's voice could be heard through the classroom door.

"Knock-knock," the voice said.

Amy looked at her students. She slowly arched her right eyebrow. But she answered in her normal voice: "Come in."

"No," said the voice. "That's *not* how it goes!"

The door cracked open a few inches. Carmen's mouth appeared through the opening.

"Let's try a do-over," she said. Then the door shut abruptly.

The students laughed.

Amy wondered why Carmen wasn't in her own class at her own school. This was very strange. She approached the door and almost opened it but then stepped back.

"Knock-knock," came Carmen's voice again.

More laughter from the students.

"Who's there?" said Amy.

"Just bacon," said Carmen.

"Just bacon who?"

"Just bacon brownies for Mother's Day."

The door opened.

Little Bartlette walked through. She was now 3 and a preschooler. She held a big, home-baked brownie decorated with a candle on a sturdy paper plate. Carmen came a step behind her.

Amy crouched down to receive the brownie and give Bartlette a big hug. Carmen, too.

Then the door opened wider.

A small grocery cart wheeled into the room, being pushed by Ferguson. The cart had cake boxes stacked in it, and a large poster hanging from its side. In stylish hand-drawn Sharpie capitals, the poster said:

THIS IS A HAPPY MOTHER'S DAY CART.
IT'S ALSO A HAPPY MOTHER'S DAY CARD.
IT IS VERY PUNNY.

BARTLETTE, FERGUSON, CARMEN & QUENTIN

Amy smiled and shook her head. One boy shouted out, “Nice double meaning!”

Then Quentin entered, carrying a disposable lighter before him like a torch. He bent over, lit the candle on the brownie, and began to sing. “Happy Mother’s Day to you…” He sang the words to the classic Happy Birthday tune. Amy stood and watched him for a few seconds. Then she closed her eyes and felt his big baritone resonating in her body.

She opened her eyes again.

As he sang, he opened the cake boxes where individual brownies already sat on small, sturdy paper plates. Neatly folded paper towels lay underneath the brownies as napkins. Quentin handed the brownies to Carmen and Ferguson to give to the students. Then Bartlette wanted in on the action. So, he promoted her to brownie delivery girl. And she did pretty well. 2 out of 3 brownies made it successfully to a student. The other one, she just sat down and ate.

When the song finished, Amy blew out the candle. And everyone applauded.

“Wow,” said Amy. She gave Quentin a hug. “I didn’t have a clue. The baking. Getting the kids out of school and day care. You were even on point with my lesson plan. Everything.”

“Not quite everything,” he said. “The kitchen’s a mess. The kids wanted to save that for you. So you felt needed.”

“Thoughtful,’” she said.

They both laughed.

Because Carmen, Ferguson and Bartlette had taken the last free chairs in the room, Amy and Quentin sat cross-legged on top of her teacher’s desk and ate their brownies there. Merry mayhem surged around them. Neither of them said a word. They just glanced to each other from time to time, their eyes bright with their own merriment.

As Amy finished her last bite of brownie, she looked down reflexively, confirming what she already knew—that the sweet chocolate treat was gone. But she didn't look up. For she saw something she hadn't expected to see.

The crumbs of the brownie spread on the white paper plate were not meaningless remnants, destined for the garbage.

They were dark stars in a constellation she recognized but could not name.

They were beautiful. They were delicious. They were hers.

She licked her index finger and ate them one by one.

"Savoring the moment?" said Quentin.

She held up the last crumb. He kissed her finger and ate the crumb in one light touch of his lips. Then they turned back to watch her students—and her children—continue to eat and play and make a complete mess of her normally tidy classroom.

It could be cleaned up later, of course.

Just like the kitchen.

Right now, Amy realized.

Right now, she thought.

Yes.

This is bliss.

www.ingramcontent.com/pod-product-compliance
Ingram Content Group UK Ltd.
Pitfield, Milton Keynes, MK11 3LW, UK
UKHW051906220426
470263UK00004B/6

9 780978 935832